This book belongs to

....

This is the story of Gingerbread Fred.

You can read it in a chair, or read it in bed.

Or you can get someone else to read it instead!

There's something else - can you guess what?

On every page there's a mouse to spot!

The Gingerbread Man

Illustrations by Sara Baker

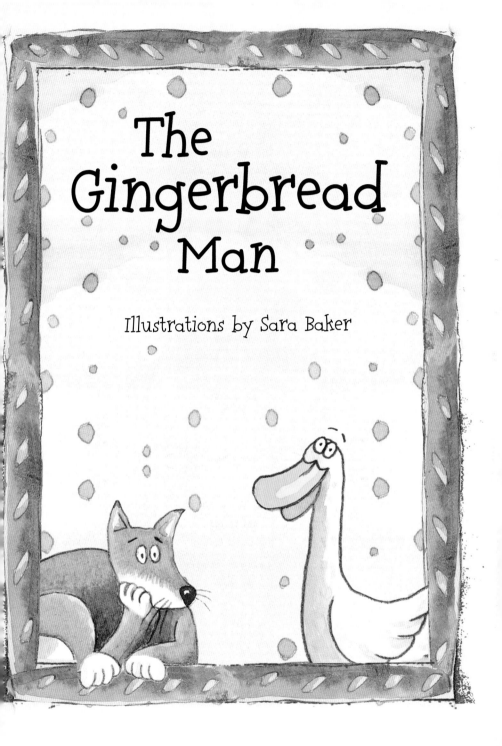

make
believe
ideas

One day, a baker and his wife make a gingerbread man who comes to life!

They name him Fred.
"Don't go out!" they say.
"You are a cookie. You
are yummy to eat!"

But Fred runs out the
door. And Fred says . . .

"Run, run, run,
as fast as you can.
You can't catch me,
I'm the gingerbread man!"

Fred reaches a garden.
There is a cat in the flowers.
"MEOW!" says the cat.
"Here comes breakfast!"

But Fred starts to skate!
And Fred says . . .

"Skate, skate, skate,
as fast as you can.
You can't catch me,
I'm the gingerbread man!"

Fred reaches a farm.
There is a dog in the barn.
"WOOF!" says the dog.
"It must be lunchtime!"

But Fred starts to ride!
And Fred says . . .

"Ride, ride, ride,
as fast as you can.
You can't catch me, I'm
the gingerbread man!"

Fred reaches a river.
A fox is sitting on the grass.
"Jump on my back," says the
fox. "I will take you across."

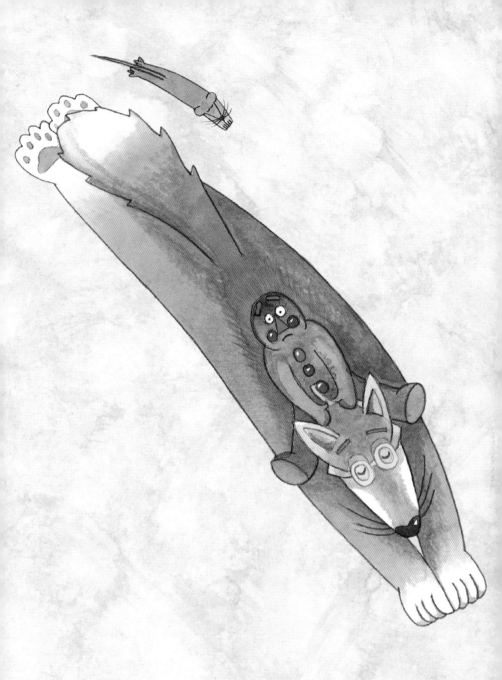

Fred rides on the fox's back!
And Fred says . . .

"Swim, swim, swim,
as fast as you can.
You can't catch me,
I'm the gingerbread man!"

The water gets
higher and higher.
"Move up and sit on
my nose," says the fox.

They reach the other side.
Fred says, "Good-bye!"
"Wait!" says the fox.
"Would you like to fly?"

The fox throws Fred
high in the sky!

And Fred says . . .

"Fly, fly, fly,
as fast as you can.
You can't catch me,
I'm the . . ."

CRUNCH! SCRUNCH! MUNCH!
The fox eats Fred for lunch.

Ready to tell

Oh no! Some of the pictures from this story have gotten mixed up! Can you retell the story and point to each picture in the correct order?

Picture dictionary

Encourage your child to read these words from the story and gradually develop his or her basic vocabulary.

baker

flowers

gingerbread man

nose

ride

river

run

skate

wife

I • up • look • we • like • and • on • at • for •

Key words

Here are some key words used in context. Help your child to use other words from the border in simple sentences.

There **is** a little old baker.

He bakes **a** gingerbread man.

"Fly as fast as you **can**."

The **dog** sees Gingerbread Fred.

Fred rides on **the** fox's back.

the • dog • big • my • mom • no • dad • all

Bake Gingerbread Fred

Ask a grown-up to help you bake Fred and his friends.
You can eat them if they look like they're running away.

You will need

4 oz butter • 3 tbsp golden molasses • 1½ cups self-rising
flour • 1–2 tsp ground ginger • ½ cup superfine sugar
• 1 egg, beaten • saucepan • mixing bowl • large spoon
• rolling pin • a gingerbread-man cutter • greased
baking sheet • colored chocolate beans • ready-made icing
in a tube

What to do

1 Turn the oven on to 350°F.
2 Melt the butter and molasses in a pan over a gentle heat.
3 Put the flour, ginger and sugar in a mixing bowl.
Add the melted butter, and molasses, stir in slightly and
then add the egg.
4 Mix the ingredients together until smooth and then
leave for 15 minutes to cool.
5 Roll out to a thickness of ¼ inch and use the cutter
to cut out the Gingerbread Fred shapes.
6 Place on the baking sheet and cook in the middle
of the oven for about eight minutes, or until golden
brown. Remove and leave to cool.
7 Decorate with icing eyes and mouth, and make buttons
from colored chocolate beans stuck on with a spot of icing.